BEYOND *my* KEEPING

BEYOND my KEEPING

Elizabeth Philips

Coteau Books

All poems © Elizabeth Philips, 1995.

All rights reserved. No part of this book covered by the copyrights hereon may be reproduced or used in any form or by any means – graphic, electronic or mechanical – without the prior written permission of the publisher. Any request for photocopying, recording, taping or information storage and retrieval systems of any part of this book shall be directed in writing to CanCopy, 214 King Street West, Suite 312, Toronto, Ontario M5H 3S6.

Edited by Patrick Lane
Cover painting by Jane Zednik, "Nightswimming," 9" x 13 1/2", oil on paper.
Author photograph by D.W. Larson
Cover design by Dik Campbell.
Book design and typesetting by Val Jakubowski.

Printed and bound in Canada.

Some of these poems have appeared in the following magazines and anthologies: *Prism, Prairie Fire, arc, Grain, event, Towards 2000* (Fifth House, 1991), *Because You Loved Being a Stranger* (Harbour, 1994), and have been broadcast on CBC's Ambience. The poems, "Meditation on Chuang-tzu," "Meditation on the Domestic," and "The Goldfish Keeper II," won an honourable mention in the Canadian National Magazine Awards.

The book, *The Natural Alien* (University of Toronto Press, 1985), by Neil Evernden was essential to the writing of some of these poems.

The author would like to thank the Saskatchewan Arts Board for their financial support and encouragement, the Saskatchewan Writers/Artists Colony Committee for retreat time, and the Saskatchewan Writers Guild for the benefits of membership. The author is grateful to Doris Larson for her critical eye, and to Patrick Lane for his tough, exacting and generous editorial advice; and she would like to thank Lorna Crozier for being there, during those hard but beautiful days in August, 1992, at St. Peter's.

The publisher gratefully acknowledges the financial assistance of the Saskatchewan Arts Board, the Canada Council, the Department of Canadian Heritage, and the City of Regina Arts Commission.

Canadian Cataloguing in Publication Data
Philips, Elizabeth

    Beyond my keeping

    Poems,
    ISBN 1-55050-077-5

I. Title

PS8581.H545B4 1995   C811'.54   C95-920021-5
PR9199.3.P454B4 1995

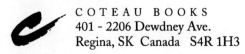

COTEAU BOOKS
401 - 2206 Dewdney Ave.
Regina, SK Canada S4R 1H3

This book is for the D.

*And in memory of
Peter McGehee and Doug Wilson*

Contents

Part One

A Gardener's Journal	*3*
Solstice	*4*
On The Road To Redberry Lake	*6*
The Water Garden	*8*
Fishkeeper's Meditation	*9*
The Goldfish Keeper	*12*
Life Of The River	*13*
The Cult Of The Head	*17*
So Red	*18*

Part Two

Leaving the Air	*21*
Letter	*22*
Old Age	*23*
Divinity	*24*
Transformation	*25*
St. Peter's, The First Day	*26*
Meditation on Botany	*28*
Balance	*30*
Stone Child	*31*
Driving Home	*33*

Part Three

Meditation On Chuang-Tzu	*37*
The Making Of Bread	*39*
Middle Earth	*42*
Snow	*44*
The Goldfish Keeper II	*46*
Meditation On The Domestic	*48*

Lake In Winter   *49*
Fields Of Care   *51*

Part Four

Praise   *55*
Seven Sacraments   *57*
Sanctuary   *64*
Medhbh Of Connacht   *65*
On The Path Of The Deer   *66*

I lingered round them, under that benign sky; watched the moths fluttering among the heath and hare-bells; listened to the soft wind breathing through the grass; and wondered how any one could ever imagine unquiet slumbers for the sleepers in that quiet earth.

–the last words of Emily Brontë

When thou hast enough, remember the time of hunger

–Ecclesiastes 18:25

Part One

A Gardener's Journal

Whatever I say must include the rose bush,
a few yellow roses open, each one imperfect, stained
brown or half-eaten by worms. The poppies, too, must be
entered, gold and orange and a single pristine white,
like this page, the sun leaving no colour behind.

Wanting to follow summer
I have taken up the pen, but have failed so far
to write anything beyond a phrase.
                            Silence
is more true to the beauty of blemished roses, the blue
haze of lobelia straining toward purple,
                            and over all
the smell of simmering green. Rows of carrots and corn
and beans throb in a bladder of light, translucent
skin of white heat. I want to capture at least the ripe
shadow of July sun, the articulate flight of the
honey bee staggering from marigold to mimulus,
preying on the tender red throat.
                            Sweating, inert,
the crown of my head burning, I sit in the garden, the seed I bear
going nowhere.

Solstice

Heat lies over the garden with the weight of oceans.
Like the thin tomato plants and long damp grass
I am caught under waves of sun, helpless
among violent orange and yellow, poppies,
marigolds bursting in the breathless afternoon.
In this steaming blaze, I ponder the world before
flowers, a constant green beneath the blue,
when water was the way and the truth,
and light fell fruitlessly on new islands, on rising
shoals and beaches.

But what I can't fathom is the will, intractable
desire, the pull to go beyond. Simple mosses
and fronds, an entire kingdom yearning
for change, conspiring after sun, the privileges of wind and earth,
the tropical rains. And how the air must have reeked
with the incense of deliberation, the ferment
at the edge of the water, plants seething
to try the drying sands of a new planet.

My ear pressed to grass, this urban ground, I listen
for that moment when the first flowers exploded severally
along the shores, their seeds conceived in air,
shaken loose and broadcast by torrential winds.
Dreaming, the hum of bees becomes
the sound of germination, new shoots breaking
out of wet earth, moving higher, away from sea-level,
blooming and dying, the surging green
future incipient in their buds.

And so, here I am, adrift on a raft of humid sun,
stuck on beginnings, our planet hanging in space
like a ripening plum. I lie on my belly, sweating
where skin touches skin, suspended
in the swing of solstice, the height of summer come too soon.
Flaring skirts of peonies and the sultry purple iris
burn around me, as I float in and out of sleep
plumbing the deep swell of light,
before the ebb, the too sudden turning.

On The Road To Redberry Lake

On the road to Redberry the sky opens and closes,
thunder and sun follow one another, descry
the changeable nature of light. The day reels
across the windshield, spectacle of candescent cloud,
sun showers, hail strung on strands of rain like a rosary
cut loose.

The fields on both sides are flooded, pools blessed
by the bent figures of migratory swans, hieroglyphs
in a forgotten tongue. They speak of a thousand miles,
generation after generation flying the routes
mapped in their cells.

The sadness of the city falls away as we sail over lush hills,
born just the other day, scoured smooth and undulant
by the shrug of a glacial shoulder. And I look to you,
driving intently in and out of rain, your face
shining, and how I love
your hands on the wheel. You steer with such care
toward the lake, the sand-flats of our escape.
You have arranged, I suspect, the phalaropes
and plovers that greet us, arrayed and crying
along the shore. We watch lightning on the horizon,
a crack appearing at the porcelain edges of a bowl.

Magician, you offer me an apricot plucked out of air.
It blushes in your palm, enclosing with such grace
the hard stone shaped like an eye, the seed
that won't see its way into the earth.

How I love your hands, tucked into your jacket pockets,
cold from the journey across the beach, searching like birds
hung on the wind, for the right move, the gesture
that will hold you back, delay the sharp descent
to the exacting ground, the common drowned fields of spring.

The Water Garden
(for Russ)

The woman who is burying her garden under water
heaves another shovelful of earth. The last pool
is almost done.

She aches at the centre
where her back strained to lift and carry children
too tired to walk. Alone now, the day almost gone

she works by moonlight and Chinese lantern.
The deep black of reflection is what she wants,
her garden pulled down into water, sky

lining the floor of each pool. The work
complete, she drags a chair into the middle of the yard.
As midnight comes on she counts five moons,
a constellation of yellow lilies. And five women
look up at her, each one with her face, her hands
lying flat in her lap

like small slices of shale, the only white
amidst the sweet green, the violent blue of summer.

Fishkeeper's Meditation

The fish come together
then diverge, a mottled orange flower
opening and closing.

Bending over the water, my shoulder-
blades grow stiff and sore, they quiver

like vestigial fins.

I do not know what a fish is –
the more I watch, the less
I know.

The fish flow on, small pockets of air
slippered in gold.

The pond is a turning world. Water sifts
through gravel, cleansing itself.

The fish feed on water fleas and algae, whatever
insects fall and are caught
on the web of the surface

while the water lilies take up what the fishes
waste.

(Creatures smaller than vision
devour
what poisons remain.)

～

The fish become water,
water becomes fish.
I am also water, though this is less
than obvious.

～

The fish are wind, they are
sky, the high corona of blue

floats down a raft of light
to lie along the face of the pool
giving the water

breath.

～

The goldfish is one of the bony fishes,
a cyprinid, a carp. But the blue oranda

is something else, a creature imagined
into life, distilled
out of moonlight, the original
florescence of snow.

～

Each summer morning I wait
for the blue fish. She rises slowly,
pewter fins

flaring. Time after time she comes to
light, a form of genesis

out of the depths,
only to sink back again, disappearing
beneath a lily pad.

I think she is not a fish
at all, but the slippery
spirit of the pond,
making heaven
out of these domestic waters.

The Goldfish Keeper

Lifting the prettiest, the slowest fish
gently into the air, just for a moment. For no reason
but to have that honour. To still her beauty
in his palm.

She lies there unmoving, her eye a small gold circle
like a child's ring. Her brief life captured
in a net of scales.

      Copper oranda,
he whispers, swim for me, and he releases her
into the water, where she comes alive again

parachuting on long billowing fins to the bottom of the pond.

Life Of The River

1.
This morning I go down to the river, silver-
green and slow, follow a school of small fish,

flurry of minnows flowing in a darting line upstream.
Though I seek their source fifty yards back

keeping pace with a slack current, the river
so low, I don't find an end, there's no last fish

beginning this abundance. Sun picks out the shoal
as if the water were not spiked with mercury,

as if the shore were not scabbed with refuse,
shards of brown glass cracking under my feet.

Those slips of blue flesh are a river of their own, going
against the body of the larger water. When I leave

I take them with me, pellucid chain, clear
as the creeks of childhood, in April

rolling through town to the beach, across cold sand
and down onto the sinking ice of the lake.

2.
One day I wear the wrong shoes, two miles down-river
I turn back barefoot, my blistered feet

stepping gingerly over sharp stones and the waiting
knives of glass. I can only glance at the river

still polishing its many-jewelled waves.
I cling instead to the dusty paths, the willows

envelope me in spidery tresses. When I reach the streets
near home, the plush boulevards

I'm relieved to have carried myself this far.
My feet have found their way, despite

years of half-hearted use, they are the fierce
pink claws of a new animal.

3.
At home, I keep the river
by me, bend

over the pond, and there
it is, that sweetness

and underneath, decay.
The water lives

because something in it
is always dying.

The pool is an eye with the river
in mind,

it takes me in
whenever I look down.

A shy fingerling
flits through my

reflection, flips
in and out of my mouth

a word I can't quite
grasp. All I catch

is the sound
fish

sibilant rain,
swift face of the river.

4.
South of an island of sand I lie down
in the current, my hands anchor me over drifted silt.

Like a merganser or teal, I receive the small
waves, pull my head under

and the river breaks in two, pouring
out of my open eyes.

Born of ice-fields hundreds of miles west, the North
Saskatchewan empties into the lake

I swam as a child. Thirty years downstream
I had despaired of that lost gift, innocent

immersion. Now, once more blessed
by water, I am no greater than any other

wafer of brightness, shadow
between shores.

The river-bottom gives way when I stand,
familiar vertigo, the inevitable fall

back into my walking body,
where I must reconcile the long drop

between the land I traverse
and the rivers flooding my heart, circular

and confined.

The Cult Of The Head

In that other place, walking was all uphill. Small wooden houses
along the curving road, the sheen of the small lake,
came into view as I laboured up the south face. Wandering
across the summit toward the field beyond the hill, it was all sky again,
mud and grass underfoot, the occasional kestrel screeching up
from the brush below. But on the prairie, I plunge
straight ahead, lungs lifting easily, a soundless
butterfly in my chest. My feet swim the grid road, propel me
toward an infinity of wheat.

Here the head comes into its own, swaying stone
flower, and I almost believe it could go on without me,
oracular, wise, draining the body of its knowledge, all blood
flowing uphill. As I walk these four miles, my head grows looser,
wobbles, wants to fly, a winged bone
with no fear of heights. Crossing a ditch deep in yellow clover,
blue alfalfa, my mind is somewhere high up, circling, a rufous
hawk scouting the ground for movement. I regret
a too stationary life if walking can get me this far,
take me back to the godhead, my own skull
a chalice for old words – sacrifice and seed, flower and bone,
fruit and libation, water and healing.

So Red

"So red," he says, taking the sweetpeas from her, and they
are, the petals darkening against the light of his blue
eyes, as he tips his face into the bouquet. This is what
she's thinking when she finds the deer later that morning,
a six-month carcass splayed beneath tall spruce
in the north field. And she remembers

the bone she'd seen somewhere, a ritual object
disinterred in Spain, a few precise lines cut
in its white surface, two hollow eyes and the lips of
the vulva, goddess of death-in-life. She has kept this image
an icon, secreted away. When she sees the deer,
ribs missing, the meat eaten and hide

cured by the elements, she sits nearby, quiet
in the solitude of that place. She stares at the slim, still perfect
limbs, delicate hooves, tawny fur tight over the bones.
Surely these legs were meant for an intricate dance
under stars. She stays half-dreaming
in the presence of the deer, rests on the mat of needles,
the wind blowing through sweet clover. When she leaves,
the fear of these last days of illness and uncertainty,
when he couldn't get out of bed and his cough shook the house,
has slipped away. The red flowers balance in her mind
with the deer, its life gone into coyote or fox,
sating the universal hunger, the invisible host.

Part Two

Leaving The Air

Barely breaking the surface of sleep, she turns
to divine the water in me, a freshet seeping from mouth
to mouth.

But I can see the dry cold light leaking in under the door
and hear the wind scything along the eaves while three months
of snow lies heavily on the ground. Sliding onto me

she urges me to swim with her, laughing and kissing me
like a fish. I smile and run my fingers
along her spine.

She begins then, her mouth creeping down my belly,
tangled hair draped over her eyes. I place my hands
lightly on her head.

The blood in my veins flickers like fins
and I am recalled to the beauty of water,
the waves pulling me

deeper. Sinking into the bed
I lose the sun and glittering snow, and soon
see only with my skin

red blanket, damp white sheet, the rest of the room
lost in fog. Drenched in the goodness of salt, my body
is blurred, littoral,

a line drawn between water and land.
My hips rise on a wave, and I'm breathing
under-sea, a pulsing eel

bearing the weight of the living water.

Letter

I watch you from where I sit at my place by the west window. You're at work in the east sun in your studio, a cloth cap pulled down over your hair. You gently lift and turn the pages of a large book (it may be that collection of Japanese prints lent us by a friend). And I wonder at the distance between our two walls of glass. I think of your sadness yesterday – your father, grown old and sick, rises in the night and pulls on his clothes, then strips them off and crawls back into bed. He keeps trying to leave for another life, the one in which he no longer waits, but acts out of the clear light of desire. But he keeps sinking back, finds himself naked in the long darkness. The weight of his last years lies like a leaden mantle along your shoulders. I want to show you this picture of yourself at work. When I look out and see you, focused and intent (you have begun to draw now), I know you've thrown aside that heaviness that might have been your inheritance, a passivity unto death. And although last night your face was pale and sore with grief, your eyes are quick now and the sunlight glances off your hands as they order the chaos of this place, this silence we have summoned between us.

Old Age

He wakes in the middle of a winter night
to a storm, except there is no storm, only the white of
years drifting in his head.

And his head whines, the wind a tightening thread
working like a screw
through the thinning flesh.

His old life rises up, the snowy expanse of fields,
still and unbroken. He sees his feet moving along the track
to the barn, walking the path

that led from one ordinary task
to another. He bends to hook a nail over a loop of rusted
wire, and then his scarred black boots

move again. The trail is routine,
no one else covers this ground, and yet he can see
from this distance, that his feet were not his own
but followed, like the deer, a course laid down
by those who have gone before. And now the mass of those
wasted days, splits apart

like an old cloud, and bitter
stars of snow
fill his mouth with dust.

Divinity

This morning, wind blowing at minus thirty, I feed a bird with a fleck of grey in a cap that should have been all black. Perched on my palm, it hooked two seeds in its beak before lifting into the air and the safety of the high branches. This may be an elder in the tribe of chickadees that inhabits this stretch of bush. A bird-god, once human, its small strength the soul of a monastic dead at the turn-of-the-century, one tuft of feathery grey hair on his naked scalp. A man who had lost his God, his faith diminishing over the years. He turned instead to the birds that passed over his hut, his cell of empty devotions. The raven, god of cold, came in the winter and sang in his throaty voice. The owl, god of the night, plundered his sleep with her obsession. Passing through in spring and autumn, the swan graced flooded fields, a question without answer. These are the last gods, I think, and though my bones ache from the cold, I hold out my hand, hoping the bird will return. I imagine the old monk, never leaving this place, not venturing beyond the end of the wood into the open field, a man who spoke to the bird, not as a god, but as a brother.

Transformation

The man clings to the sheer face of the mountain
in a storm of ice, while his friend, attached to him
by an umbilicus of blue cord, is trapped below,
silenced by a massive sheet of water turned to stone.

The man knows what he has to do with the time left
before the rising gale obscures the life-saving
path of descent. He must cut the rope
and save the others who call out in answer to his call.

Just as knife severs rope, tight and cold
as a steel cable, he hears a cry
and a raven rises out of the crevasse, pure jet
against the blank of spinning snow,
bird of darkness, leaving the body of earth
for the body of air, flying headlong
into sky. Rising on black wings,

we tear the white mask off the face of the rock.

St. Peter's, The First Day

1. Morning
Halfway along the path I stop and listen to snow sifting through a net of black branches; reach up and pocket a tamarack fruit, its whorled florets sere and brittle as a pine cone.

The trees are mostly poplar, a few larch, and the odd pine, its trunk mapped in purple and ochre, exotic in this world bleached white and grey.

I feed a handful of raw seeds to chickadees gathering in nearby boughs. One by one they land, tilt their heads as if gauging the pulse in my palm, grasp a seed and fly off, leaving my hand

both lighter and heavier than before. I can't guess at the weight of so small a bird, ballast for a torn strand of wind. I look up as a sudden

careening flight of waxwings raises and lowers the pale corners of the sky.

2. Late afternoon
On the road near the Abbey, I meet one of the hermits shovelling someone's car out of a snowbank. Rumour says he's sworn to a lifetime of silence. As we push on the rear bumper, he and I lean our shoulders into it, the tires humming, spitting grey grit, as I rest and he shovels out the front wheels, and we push again, the car rocking like a boat, he never stops talking. About how many times his truck has been stuck like this, the walking back in minus forty weather, his beard turned to ice. About this strange winter, cold then warm then cold, and about his new dog, the same only younger than his old one. When the car finally surges out of the snow, he falls heavily in the dirty ruts, but leaps up grinning. He crosses himself, thanks God for one more deliverance from snow.

3. Evening
I bathe and put on clean clothes,
sit down to receive the last half hour of light.

The sky blazes, fleetingly radiant, still labouring
out of the black well of winter solstice. Here

solitude begins. Night swells
and the mind falls back on itself.

I retrieve the dry seed, rosette of a larch
out of season, and find it broken
into a wooden sprig – precisely cruciform
in bloom.

Meditation On Botany

1.
The tamarack, also known as the hackmatack, is a conifer,
an important colonist when the earth was newly green,
pioneering the farthest and highest reaches of dry land.

There was a time when the conifers held sway over the world,
a landscape darkened by fir and pine, juniper and cedar.

The ground thick with cones, each scattering a million grains of pollen,
profligate naked seeds.

Holding the cone of a tamarack, dry brown rosebud,
the woman tries to imagine that time.

The sun, millions of years younger, still conjuring
fruit. The wind scoured clean by the gin-bright
breathing of evergreens.

2.
The tree has a single living layer, this she knows
as cambium. A pipe only one cell thick,

it flutes out of the ground
the tree's provender.

The woman looks at her hands and thinks how still
she would stand if she had only one vein,
and how straight.

And winter would come, a ruthless gift
bestowing silence.

She envies the tree those months of rest, when thin
ridges of snow soften the stark lines of branches, the tree
empty as a buddha.

3.
Cross-legged beneath the tamarack
the woman is hard at work, the needles above her
autumn yellow as the tree withdraws into sleep.
She reaches up and strokes a feathery
bough, *it feels like the hair of an angel,*
she thinks. Then shakes her head, that's not it.
Like the hair of a child –

but no, she must try harder. Closing her eyes
she sinks deeper, the tips of her fingers
rest lightly on the damp ground.
The glow of the tamarack
aches in her head.

Like the hair of that boy! and she remembers how he sang to her, his voice hoarse, just on the verge of breaking. A small girl, she clung to his back as he pedalled through the streets. Out long after dark, she should have been home in bed, she should have been afraid, but that night was made of soft whole cloth, and it dropped gently among the elms. He was a stranger, come out of nowhere and singing. His long blond hair was brittle as grass, his hands were rough and chapped, and they bled easily.

4.
The tree sheds its needles, red
sleet. The woman
dozes, her head empty.

Balance
(in memory of Fusi, childhood friend)

This is the journey. I drive from the city to the small town of my birth, spend the first night in my childhood bed, in the province where I was born. I leave early the next morning, not wanting to pass the house of my friend, where the land backs on the water, the water where he drowned last week, he and his father both, fishing on the lake just free of winter's ice. In the morning I get in the car and drive east, a thermos of coffee on the seat beside me, and one of my mother's sandwiches in a paper bag. I am going to visit my friend who has moved away. Travelling beyond Thunder Bay and up, around Lake Superior, over the rugged hills, I pass through a landscape part real and part imagined, the road flying through my head, rasping wind of a long journey blowing my mind clear. I put in two long days, bearing myself deeper and deeper into solitude, hanging onto the wheel, sleeping in the car those few black hours in the middle of the night. It's after one in the morning when I finally arrive, surprising my friend and her husband, waking them up. I accept a glass of beer, and we talk around the kitchen table, in the preternatural calm of late night, the air wafting in the window as warm as true summer. Just before going to bed, I step in to see their twelve-month child. His dark head vivid against the white sheet, his mouth serious, working at sleep. *This is the destination.* I touch the unfurling fern of his fist, and before I too lie down to rest, I wish him balance, the gift of keeping any boat, skiff or sail, upright on the sharp waves of an early morning in spring.

Stone Child

A stone survives
summers of monastic
quiet, eternal

ceilings of snow, then
one August morning
snags my foot crossing

the dry slough. This
is worth digging out,
I surmise, and do so

rubbing down
the subdued, almost
amethyst brown, the

surface covered with pale
scars where light breaks
out of the inner

recesses.
The stone is cleft
at the centre

where another rock
struck
during the slow glacial

tumult. The rosy wound
is rough, though the rest
is silk, patina of great

patience.
Too much for one hand
to bear easily, I walk

the stone awkwardly
home. Slaking my thirst
with ice water

I cradle the lithic
child in my lap, a
work of sun

and pressed clay,
unearthed. It's perfect
weight, darkness verging

on the sexual,
enjoins me to love
what's better left

unopened, the silence
building
and building.

Driving Home

I want to say something about fear, and yet encompass
the light last night, driving home through dusk, through August,
the fields transfixed beneath a rusty blue light, the hills falling away
from the car like a sea
subsiding.

I want to say something about my casual grip on the wheel,
my body subdued after miles of winding road.
How I could have left it then, easily, failing to make the turn. I had that
chance. To abandon the body, the burden of its will,
in a slough where the road dips sharply to the right.

I saw myself lying in cat-tails and marsh grass,
a slight wind stirring the reeds. And I longed for that unnatural silence,
after the engine failed and the car sank
into the bog. Before the blackbirds and frogs
resumed their singing.

But by fear or instinct, I kept to the road, and arrived
safely, despite the dread of arriving, the loss
that must come after. I reached the city, still basking
in the blush of the darkening land, though the cold night
congealed around me.

And I was ashamed then of merely passing through, scarcely knowing
the terrain. Because I did not stop
and walk up the hills, not even at the Shrine of Our Lady
of the Sorrows, where the prospect
is surely sacred.

I did not stop and touch rocks piled in the fields,
where the heat of the day lingers,
though I might have found a stone of megalithic grace,
a plinth to mark my doorway. Caught in the momentum of the
machine, I drove without stopping.

I parked the car and sat down on the grass by my gate,
reluctant to go in. I wanted to remain in the open, where the hush that fell
with the last light across the hills, and the sweep of sky,
were so generous, even I, traversing my own
landscape of fear, found benediction.

Part Three

Meditation On Chuang-tzu
(for Patrick)

The goldfish I have called
Chuang-tzu, after the Chinese sage,
chases along the surface of the water
sifting for scraps of food.
Isolated from the school by sickness,
by grey threads of fungus
that grow on his fins like mold
on bread, he is confined to five gallons,
a clump of java moss, gravel
and one smooth black stone.

Even in sickness he is full-
hearted, swims a spiral dance
carving out of water
his own kingdom, a world without
edges. He sucks greedily there
balanced on the sweeping
butterfly of his tail, catching
small mouthfuls of bright air.
The medicine has failed to cure him
and yet he grows, a stout
gleaming oranda, each scale
a finely etched oval of bronze light.

From my desk where I read
Chuang-tzu, I look up as the oranda
plunges to the bottom, shimmying hard
then resting, only to float up again
effortlessly, like a balloon
let go.

Chuang-tzu says, "if water is clear
when it is tranquil, how much more so
the spirit?" And I imagine him,
an old man straying into a strange wood,
distracted, on a new path.
Surprised by the pool at his feet
he stops and peers down at his own face
reflected. His eyes
are two perfect moons, and he sees in them
the stillness he has been seeking
all his life, an emptiness
to which all things must gravitate.

But then the goldfish, the life of the pond,
rise to meet his shadow, shattering
his moment of vision, sight
distorted once more
by the roiling spirit of the water,
tame fish wild in hunger and the light
on the water broken, refracted
by the swift congregation of fish
stirring as one body, one
open mouth.

The Making Of Bread
(for D.)

1.
Water, just a few degrees warmer
than the body, and a little sugar
to help the yeast work. This is how
bread begins. The first stirring of appetite

is the smell of yeast as it foams.
In the ancient kitchens of France, where bread
has baked every morning for hundreds of years,
the spores of yeast live in the air,

and all that's needed to start the souring
is flour and water. This is a marriage
that works. I imagine taking my bowl of stone-
ground wheat, my cup of water

down to our room on a Sunday morning, the high
ferment of our marriage still simmering
there in the cloistered air
over the unmade bed.

2.
After the folding and punching and turning,
my hands gritty with flour, the dough begins
to breathe. I rest my palms on the leaven round
and remember your belly rising, the small

loaves of your breasts, tang of salt
on your nipples. I place the dough
in a large greased bowl. My love, I want always

to be your baker.

3.
I cover the bowl with a white cloth
starred with blue flowers, a piece cut
from a tablecloth of my grandmother's.
She's dead fifteen years now, yet I hear
her voice as I bend to the oven.

I am surrounded by women. I can hear you, my lover
of seven years, talking in another room. I bake bread
so you will love me
even more. I like to watch

your dark lips open to taste the steaming
slice. And so the work of my hands
becomes your body.

4.
An hour later the dough has risen, filling
the bowl. I love punching it down, that moment
when it subsides, the held breath
released. How like the engorged clitoral rose

after love – the blood flows back into the body
and that pungent flower fades. O the foolish
comparisons I might make, between women
and bread, the luscious sourdough of our bodies

always keeping back enough unfinished
leaven. It is true
that after I've ascended the almost unbearable heights
and then fallen away
from pleasure, my too ravenous
flesh soon rises again. As you know,
my love, all it takes is a deft
second kneading.

5.
The loamy incense of bread just out of the oven
wafts through the rooms of our house like sunlight
baking the clay on the first day of creation.
Inhale deeply, my love, as you enter, coming in

out of the snow. You have arrived. Lie down with me now
and allow me the embrace of the beautifully braided
muscles of your arms. Bread
is cooling on the rack.

When we are done, we'll make a meal of it,
sate our other appetite, and the round will be complete.
Hunger, pleasure, ful-
fillment, this is the baker's wheel.
As our mouths make circles of all flesh,
I can barely wait for this pleasure to end,
so in love am I with beginning, the heavy dough
kneaded until it shines, and we rise again

into hunger.

Middle Earth

In our garden a purple anemone is open, hardy petals furred against late frost. I step back from this contained fire

to weigh the effort it will take to revive this piece of ground after last year's devastation, the digging of the goldfish pond and laying of pipe. I try to locate orange

lilies, poppies, delphinium, the best angle, clearest view of goldfish schooling and scattering. These are the pleasures

I must answer to. As I stand, my body is in its moment, breasts painful under the pressure of time, cells gravid

with the waters of the uterine moon. I am also the fertile body, my flesh groaning – a burden that repeats and resounds

through the middle of life – caught in a cycle that ends in barrenness, in the flowering blood. The demands of cultured

earth are plain enough, topsoil and black-rotted manure must be laid on, a little peat dug in around the perennials. We'll spend a whole day

wheeling barrows of humus, our shoulders throwing the spade deep into a movable feast of fine black soil. But although we swagger like gods

over this narrow lot, we are humbled by the splayed red tulips in their abandon, evening's spectral light thrown off by new sparks of grass, a green singing

scored out of the mouth of spring. I number my labours as I stand weary in this woman's body, and yet float free, lifted out of ripeness by a power I cannot know, as my womb clenches in its turn, swollen sheath, hopeful pod

bursting with impossible fruit.

Snow
(for Doug)

I look out at the ruin of the garden, draped now in snow
bestowed by a generous wind, and I see the pond

suspended under pebbled ice, papery tongues of a bulrush trembling,
caught in iron-grey morning light.

On a wooden trellis one last flower clings to the tip of the
clematis, a pinky-red star

and I take a deep breath

for last glories, the red sky of late July
condensed into this constellation, failing fast

over a glistening bay of snow. And I think of my friend
who stayed on his feet until he lost his balance

just weeks before the virus took him.
It was never the simple joys he sought, but the uncommon

happiness of a man who could sing,
who could get a whole room of people singing

Amazing Grace in the dark. The sound was like mourning, a communal
grief made beautiful. It is this memory

that comforts me, having been there, partaking
in an ancient keening, a song so essential to me

I never could have found it on my own. And now
in the mild twilight, I hang on to joy

in the sensuous drifts, light doubling back on itself,
resonant between the low ceiling of cloud and this first

immaculate fall of snow.

The Goldfish Keeper II

His oldest fish, ten years old, the shubunkin
is beyond recovery, bloated, eyes bulging,
its field of vision opened up by pain.

Netting the fish, he places it on the cement floor
and brings his hammer down in one smooth sharp blow
to the back of its head. He rinses the blood away
and drops the body into the wood-stove.

Comfortable in this, he's grieved by how easy
it is; he goes on steadily
to the next chore.

It's only in the evening, waiting for sleep
that he sickens. Sees the hammer
coming down and the life
blasted out, a skinful of guts
left behind.

The fish swims back into his mind, flashing silver
and blue, her tail kicking against the green
surface of the pool.

He tosses in his bed, recalling other
necessary deaths, the colours
school in his mind. Red and gold, orange and bronze,
calico.

~

He remembers each fish in turn, the bright dance
they made, their shadows in summer
guttering ghosts on the walls of the pond.
The years he tended them, the buckets filled
and emptied, the food

scattered like an offering onto the water.

~

He drifts in and out of dream, sees the blue fish
gone wild again, thrashing,
an ancient carp struggling to break free.

The night deepens around him but the fish
won't let him go. Trapped with him
on the edge of sleep, she measures
in fierce strokes
the limits, the end of his care.

~

When the first light streaks the window
she slows to her old pace, and he's calmed,
soothed again by her rhythm.

Falling asleep now, he watches, relieved
as she sinks into the clean cold water
beyond his keeping.

Meditation On The Domestic

The fish climb the column of bright water, hexagonal
pillar of false sun in the heart of the house, below ground.
This is where we gather in the evening, we go down
into the basement and wait for the fish – orandas, fantails,
and one black moor – to do their work. We shed the day, the grey
skin of the city, as the goldfish glide in and around
spikes of eel grass, soft spirals of cabomba. The fish
rise and fall along ropes of moving water, riding the pulley of forced
air, bubbles breaking across the surface like stars.

Veiled in long fins, exaggerated, rare,
the goldfish have been bred for splendour, spun from
centuries of fish dreams, the human mind casting itself back
into the sea. The fish weave their colours into the water,
skeins of blood-red and orange, silver and blue. Only the moor
is alone in its darkness, leaving the others
her share of light.

Lying on the floor, we look up through the glass at the fish mirrored once,
twice, three times. Caught in the illusion
we believe for a moment in the gills that grant us passage
through the perilous depths of sleep. Captured by the fish,
their careless dance, we are released again into water,
a heaviness our limbs desire (messengers
from our first world, the fish swim toward us
out of our own blood).

Lake In Winter

I walked the frozen crust of shore, twelve years old
and still amazed by evening, by blue-black
sky nailed up with stars. I remember the cold
singing in me as I drank in the cutting edge of air
and stepped out onto the ice. I walked till the lights of town
were small behind me, and what lay ahead
was not the other shore, but darkness, massive
and true.

Out there, nothing but ice and snow, the alluring
lines of distance. I lay down then
and considered the fish
swimming beneath me, somnolent and grey.
I'd seen fish caught and hauled up out of the ice,
had seen them drown, tails fighting
air, the blue sunlight
that was to us the saving grace of winter.

I imagined a school of perch below me, yellow stripes
faded, eclipsed by the ice I leaned against, a wall
between worlds. Depending too much on water
transfixed, I was shaken when the floes
shifted, unseasonable thunder
under my back. A gap had opened in the ice
beside me, and I knew then I had come too far.
I stood, stunned as my heart

emptied. I ran for shore, my breath
tearing silence. On the beach again, I told myself
I might have dreamt that noise, herald of change
and treachery. But there was no denying
where I'd been, strayed beyond some border
to where the ice breaks when the water
moves, the lake
bucking like a body on the threshold of sleep.

Fields Of Care

My heart is north, pure
navigation, an abiding source
to guide you home. Inside,
the arterial forest surges
with the great herds, caribou
and moose and the attendant wolves
procuring mercy.

My eyes are east, always rising
to the light. They see the world spin
through space like a single cell, blue
drop of rain on night glass, spider
in a web of stars.

My tongue is south, singing
long hot days soaked in sun,
and oranges swelling. Fed on groundwater
the oranges
ripening.

My breasts are here, night after night
they govern the soft confines of sleep.
The west is all darkness, succour,
a full belly, rest.

I offer my body as a map. Accept me.
Taste the river in my mouth, the fish
in my blood.

Read the lines on my palms
drawn by the feet of sparrows. They are the thin
veins of leaves, the gorges and glacial faults
converging in the sea.

I offer you the body. Revere the aging skin
as it falls away, the settling bones.
They will take you home,
truly. Follow the body down, go slowly
and with deference to your place, some wild field,
and lie down
easy in your last bed of earth.

Part Four

Praise

I have chosen the moment of the flowering crab,
this crowd of white blossoms I stand beneath,
to address you, the audience I take on faith.
In my backyard in a small city on the Prairies
I pray for stillness, for abstinence, a fall
from desire. Alone in my garden with the nascent
grass of spring softly stirring,
I face you.

I confess to the sins of our age. I have conspired
at death, decrease, contamination. I have gorged
on more than my fair portion, trusting the illusion of plenty.
Supported by law and dominion, my guns
have brought down geese, marring the perfect
vee of the southbound flock, ending courtships
and ancient lines.

Do not mistake me. I acknowledge the name of predator,
that awful necessity. But at the same time have renounced
the place where all forgiveness lies – I have walked
without supplication, without paying fealty to the ground,
the still gorgeous earth.

I have denuded whole hillsides of virgin forest
wielding a chainsaw, the whining insatiable teeth.
My hands have gone numb and yet I have not given up
the machine. I have conferred and denied blessing
with the touch of a finger, saying this is mine
and therefore sacred, and this I cast off.
And I have not loved what I have thrown away.
I confess to believing in the technological conceit,
the deft death-defying sleight of mind.

I know you must scorn this confession, a too easy
penance. That you will shun as I have done, the mother
planet, and seek to shield yourself from the coming and going
of our distant father, the sun. Blinded by rebellion, suffering
from a distracted, adolescent gaze, we are all
of an age.

Here beneath this apple tree
I beseech you. Learn with me to praise our sister,
citizen of sweetness, and remember the tart fruit,
the harvest. Say after me, *thou*
tree of life, tree of wisdom,
tree of knowledge, tree of mercy.

Seven Sacraments

1.
Take and eat this
in honour of fruit borne out of the deep

oven of summer
pluck the perfect round from the vine

still warm from long sun, red
after the lash of August winds

and taste in each blushing cell
blessed rain, the fall of

water stained ochre in the holy
crucible of storm

take this in your mouth (your mouth
the vessel of sacrament)

and savour the elemental
taste, salt-

sweet of summer's blood
for this is the earth

made flesh
and do not abstain, nor deny the moment

when fruit is ripe and heavy to hand
bite down through the tight peel

cherish the sudden rush of juice
the near-drowned tongue

2.
To the gorgeous sleepy gods of the grove,
bending rowans, languid
under boughs laden with orange berries

To the square of bare ground
beneath the floating crown of horse chestnut
its hard unripened lobes

To the rare stillness
there, unfolding petals of leaf-
sanctified dark

To this hallowed place of waiting
I pray

for a dying fall:

*may my hands tremble, loosing
their hold on the spavined
trunk of the pine*

*may I slowly and without sorrow
let go
fistfuls of torn gold and russet bark*

*as I collapse through the quickening
shadow, sharp musk
toward a final absolution*

*where my lips, my mouth
have nothing but joy
to confess*

in the silence, the coming to rest
along the dusky shoulder of the earth

3.
She partakes in the sacrament of the stone
when she is light and dry
like straw, the autumn sun in pale tatters

at her feet. She needs the weight
to hold her down, to carry in her pocket
like a talisman. She wants a stone

that halts the light before it goes to ground.
A smooth sphere, its contours as familiar
as her own body.

She dreams of a stone as fragile and lucid
as a blackbird's egg, and in its heart
the molten core of the earth.

She hones her understanding – colour and form
give meaning to her hand. A bone is also stone.

In the field, she bends to uncover
the vertebra of a calf, and feels the pull of that link
ripple along her own spine.

Clay is a book of stone, its gold pages
inscribed with the remains of leaves,
the flight of ancient moths.

Wood is stone that hardens
refusing death.

Water is the last stone, the only one
she cannot hold, slipping through her fingers
with an unattainable grace.

It is water she wants most, in its clear eye
mineral salts linger, essential
traces of memory.

4.
In the white cloister of winter, rites are brutal
but few. High cold walls close in, and stay
desire.

Walk slowly beneath birch and ash,
the silence of trees, their branches like flutes
empty of breath, green song
forsaken.

Go out to meet the first wild storm
and hold, with hands bared, the bitter
chalice of the air.

Forget the blood, steaming in shallow skeins
beneath the skin, and follow the eye
the lines of snow, the massive
net of descending sky.

Witness how even the coldest season bends
and worships, drawn down
and down

to lie enchanted
along the ground.

5.
When the first shoots of grass, tender fringe of green,
emerge from under the retreating hedge of snow,
her body grows heavy, swollen
with a genital sadness.

Even the promise of her garden, the long-awaited sowing,
is a burden, its poor soil another constraint
on a brief season. She lies down in the evening
and grief roots in her.

When she must go out she veils herself in feigned
joy, her smiles cracking like the panes of ice lining the lane,
but no one notices, their faces tipped away from her
to the heat of the resurrected sun.

Each spring, she must force her way out, seeking in dreams
redemption, release from the barren place
her body knows. After days of too much sleep, the stale
smell on her skin won't wash away.

One night she dreams a half moon
lodged inside her, waxing. She wraps herself in a thick robe,
trying to eclipse that harsh
light, as wave after wave of pain sweeps through her

then seeps away, leaving her curled around
the instant of relief, until it builds again – the stolen light of the sun
almost splitting her in two. When morning dawns, the sky
polished to pearl by rain, she finds her thighs anointed

by dark oil, the blood sacrament. Lowering her face
into the greasy bowl of her hands, she weeps
and weeps, the humid spring air pouring in the window
like forgiveness, like mercy.

6.
She shakes the fine black seeds into her palm, sleeping
cells of an articulate dust
gleaned from the sweetest of last summer's crop.

Cupping her hand so the wind will not scatter them, she lifts
her face to the mist.

She has been out all day
digging row after row, working the ground –
bending, standing, bending. This is the old
intimacy, eyes trained on the loam at her feet,
the slash of trowel and hoe

while her mind restrains her hands, damping down
the urge to take too much, give too little.

The clouds part and a tall sun
suffuses new grass with the copper of an ancient
alchemy, but she does not stop

to admire the garden, briefly gilded. Hands deep
in the rough trough of earth, she pauses only
after she has let go the waiting life.

The world comes down to this
small act of sacrament, straining after
balance, sowing the well-tilled soil.

She bows her head again, and feels along her nape
a cold spark, the first sepal of rain.

7.
A stream wells up to meet me as I gain the world of sleep,
burgeons to a river that converges on the much-
dreamt place of childhood, source of purpose, source of
pleasure – lake without end.

Water rises as I fall, the only land a mirage
along the eastern shore. Lulled by slow waves
I am recalled to an evening in late summer
when the lake

and the mild light lie together, softness
on softness, and I float on my back,
my flesh become the world – hands and feet stretch
far away, almost to the horizon

my breath swells in and out, and I drift
and drift through the day
toward the culmination, when all failing
is washed away, the hour

condensed into an entire summer's baptism.
I move then, turning with the water, stroking, turning,
and each time I surface, my eyes open
into the polished half-shell of sky above the lake where I was born.

Sanctuary

Since she was a child she has come often to this gully
beside the railway tracks, where she is engulfed
by shoulder-high thistle, swaying purple globes

crowning thorny stalks. Around her ankles
a clump of foxtail brushes bare skin. These are the familiar
among unknown weeds

and grasses, the nominal, the useless.
Walking this margin, this fragment of prairie,
she loses the voices of the city,

the arguments, the lies. In the distance
she can hear the shunting of cars, huge vessels
loaded with wheat and gas and chemicals. She wishes

the ditch were as broad as a valley, wishes she could hear
no sound beyond her own careful steps and the low
frenzy of bees. Then she might go far enough afield

making her escape. Perhaps
somewhere a gate has been left open,
a gap in the wall, and if she lets go,

a body running blind along the bottom of the gorge,
she might just slip through.

Medhbh Of Connacht

I am telling you about Medhbh of Connacht
that wild Celtic queen who led armies against Ulster
and whose appetites

were legion. She said
she was never without one man
in the shadow of another

and as I speak
your breast is the shadow of my breast
and my hip is the shadow of your hip

and my hand, so much smaller than your hand,
moves toward the shadow of

your belly, and I am forgetting Medhbh
of Connacht whose shadows were legion

as your other mouth becomes the shadow
of the shadow
of my mouth

until we are both gone
into the darkness
upon darkness

without men.

On The Path Of The Deer

I am following the path of the deer through spruce
and down into pine, glimpsing now and again the blue
flash of a jay flapping from tree to tree.

I am going deeper into the wood on a trace hammered sound
by the passing of hooves, to the place
where seven beds are pressed out of the snow, seven hollows

glazed by the warm bellies of sleeping deer. I take the path
away from the quiet hall where last summer my friend
called after me and laughed

and caught me up. But he never followed me here,
never saw the marks where soft mouths of deer have grazed
the tender bark of young trees.

His long stride never left me breathless
beneath this sprawling pine. I am tracking the way of the deer
beyond the range of his beckoning on the day that I turned

and met his green gaze. And yet
I hear him ahead of me now, his feet singing on the trail
in the twilight of the trees, and though I go with great care

I cannot catch him up. His laugh hovers in the air
above the last bend, and surely I will not be lost
or without blessing if he allows me

to see him just this once leaping after the deer on the path
that leads to sleeping in circles of snow in the heart
of the wood.

Elizabeth Philips

Elizabeth Philips is the author of two previous books of poetry, *Time in a Green Country* (Coteau Books, 1990) and *Breaking Through Ice* (Turnstone, 1982). Her poems have been published in several literary magazines, including *Malahat Review, event, Arc, Prism, Prairie Fire* and *Grain*. Her work has also been included in the anthologies *Heading Out* (Coteau, 1986), *Toward 2000* (Fifth House, 1990) and *Because You Loved Being a Stranger* (Harbour, 1994).

Born in Winnipeg and raised in Gimli, Manitoba, Elizabeth has lived in Saskatoon since 1980. She has been involved with the collective that publishes *NeWest Review* and was editor of Grain in 1993-94.

About the cover artist

Born in Toronto in 1953, Jane Zednik has studied at Mount Allison University, York University, the University of Saskatchewan and the Banff Centre. Since 1980 she has had over a dozen solo exhibitions and her work has appeared in a number of group exhibitions in western Canada, Ontario and Newfoundland. Her paintings have also been purchased for a number of public collections across the country by corporations, museums and other institutions.